challenging
mazes
80 timed mazes to test your skill!

Illustrated by Lisa Mallet
& Marc Parchow

Text by Elizabeth Golding
Designed by Anton Poitier & Ben Potter

BARRON'S

D1279116

First edition for the United States
and Canada published in 2016 by
Barron's Educational Series, Inc.

This book was conceived, created,
and produced by iSeek Ltd.
Copyright © iSeek Ltd. 2015

Illustrated by Lisa Mallet &
Marc Parchow
Text by Elizabeth Golding
Designed by Anton Poitier & Ben Potter
Chief Maze Tester: Sophia Langdon

All inquiries should be addressed to:
Barron's Educational Series, Inc.
250 Wireless Boulevard
Hauppauge, New York 11788
www.barronseduc.com

ISBN: 978-1-4380-0788-5

Library of Congress Control
Number: 2015940579

Date of Manufacture:
January 2016
Manufactured by: Zhong Tian
Colour Printing Co., Ltd.,
Panyu, China

Printed in China

9 8 7 6 5 4 3 2

Be Amazing!

This book is jam packed with amazing mazes, which start easy and get harder as you go through the book. Every maze has a time challenge for you to beat. Look out for the clock at the top of each maze, which is in minutes and seconds:

BEAT THIS!

`01:20`

Use a watch with a second hand, or a mobile phone timer to check your time from starting to finishing each maze. You could write down your time on each page.

Find the start point for each maze by looking for a red arrow:	Find the end point for each maze by looking for a blue arrow:

Some of the mazes go across the fold in the book. There are tips with these mazes to explain how to get across from one side of the page to the other.

To complete each maze, it's a good idea to use a pencil and to have an eraser handy in case you go the wrong way. Solutions are on pages 87-96 in case you get really stuck.

On your mark, get set, go!

Don't get lost in this pretty village.
Try to beat the clock!

Fly along the branches of this tree!

How many birds do you pass on the way?

These guys are weird! Can you get past them?

BEAT THIS!
00:45

Help the ants feed their queen!

BEAT THIS!
00:50

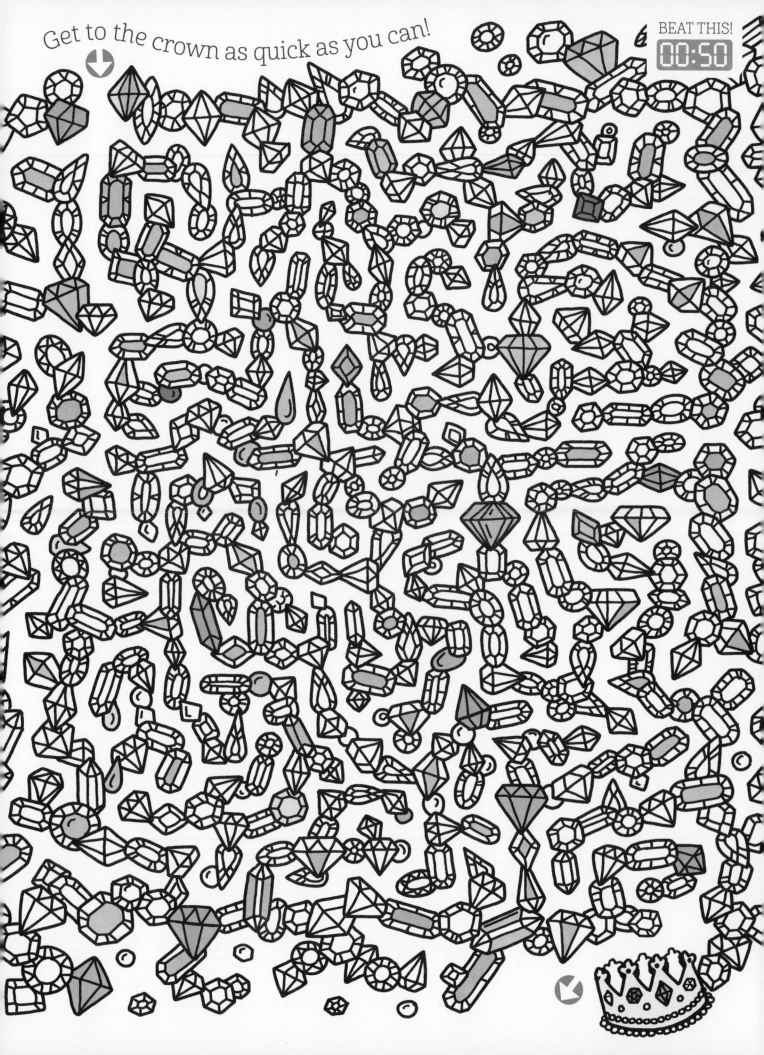

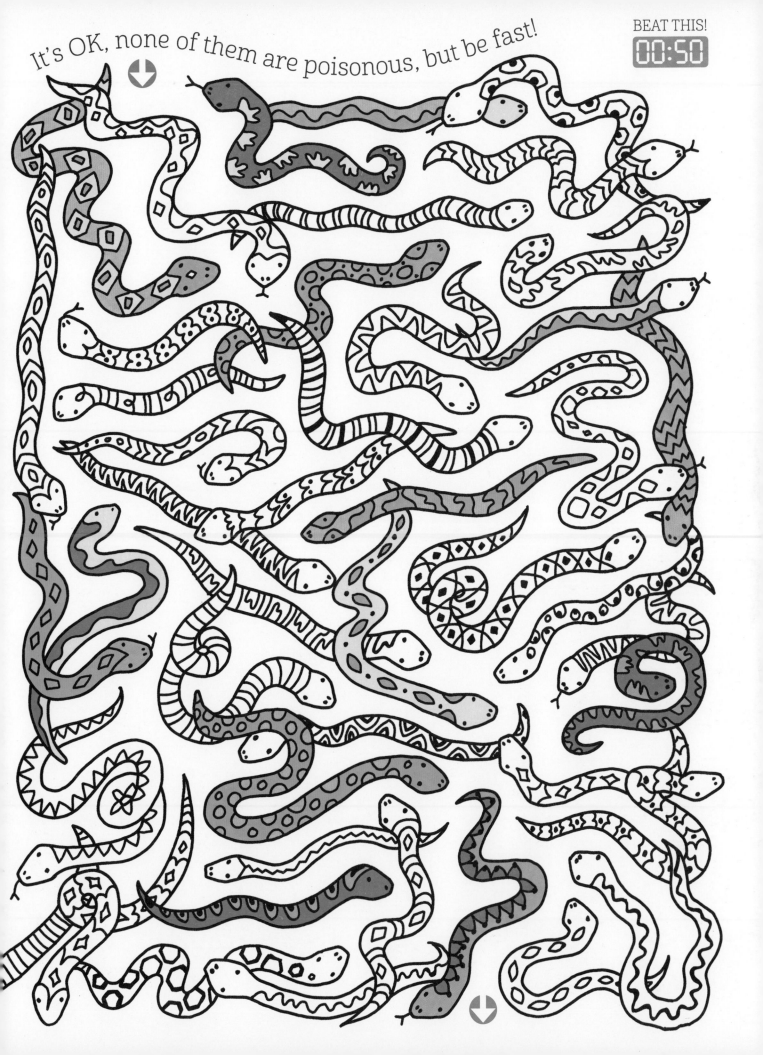

Don't get trampled! Did you pass a yellow elephant?

Which way to the pearl? Take your pick!

BEAT THIS!
01:00

Find a way through!

BEAT THIS!
01:00

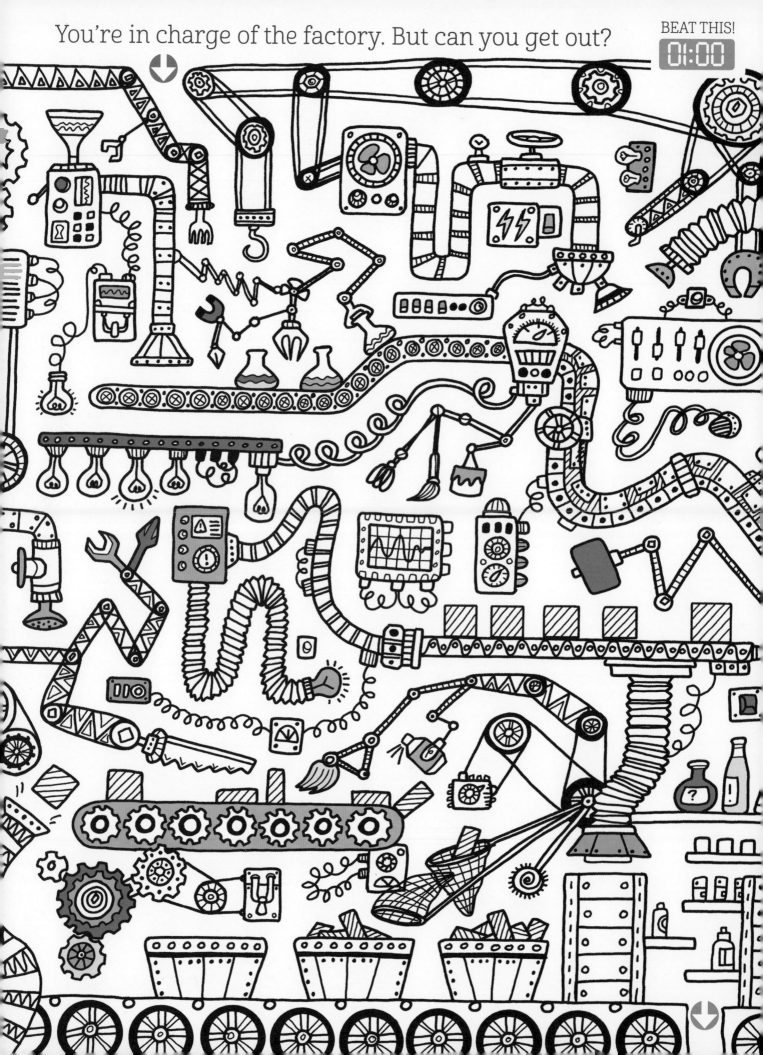

Guide the rabbit home to his hole.

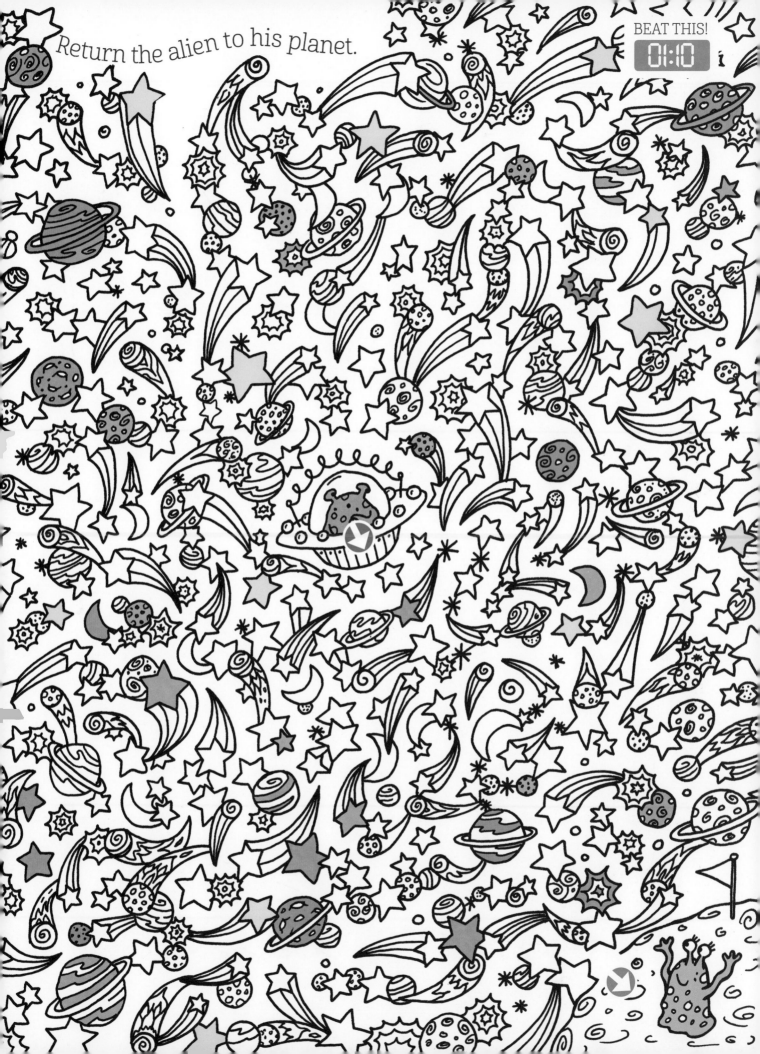

Return the alien to his planet.

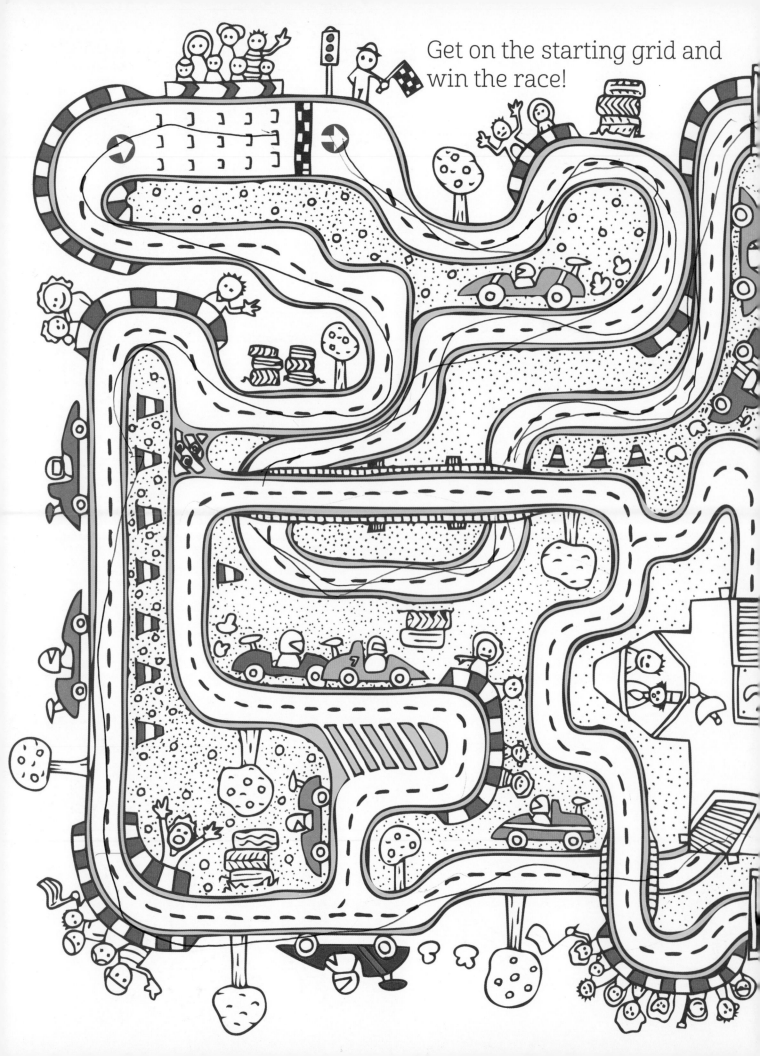

Get on the starting grid and win the race!

Let's get out of here!

Only one plug is for the lamp. But which one?

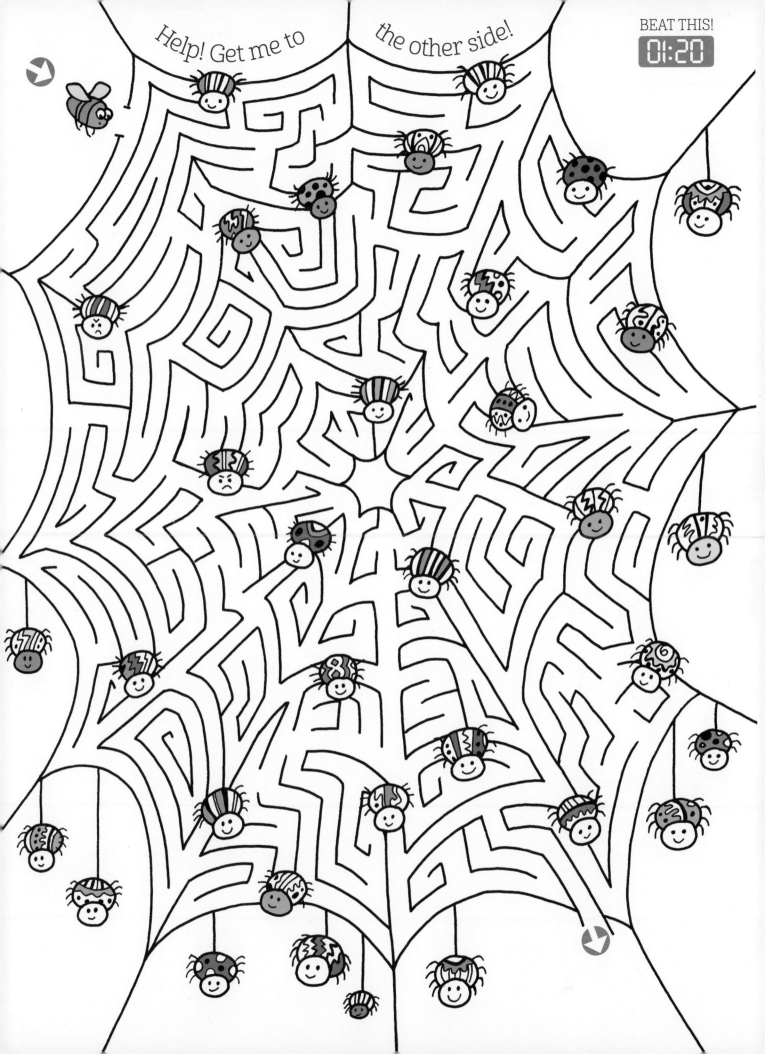

Help! Get me to the other side!

BEAT THIS!
01:20

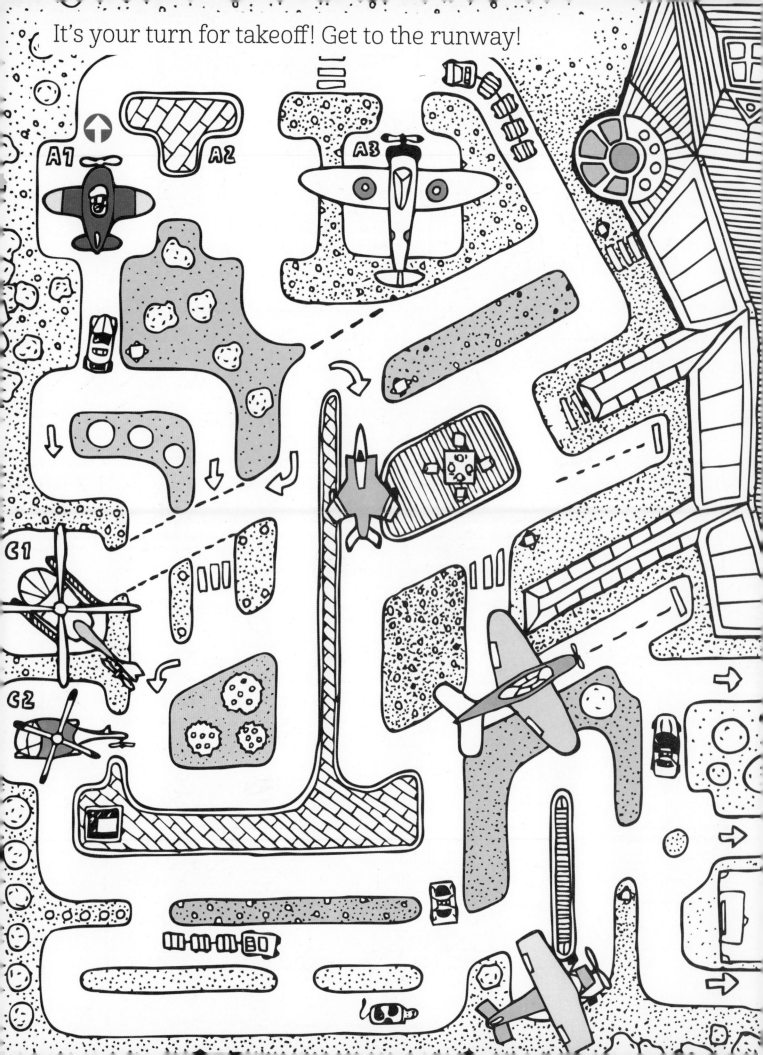

It's your turn for takeoff! Get to the runway!

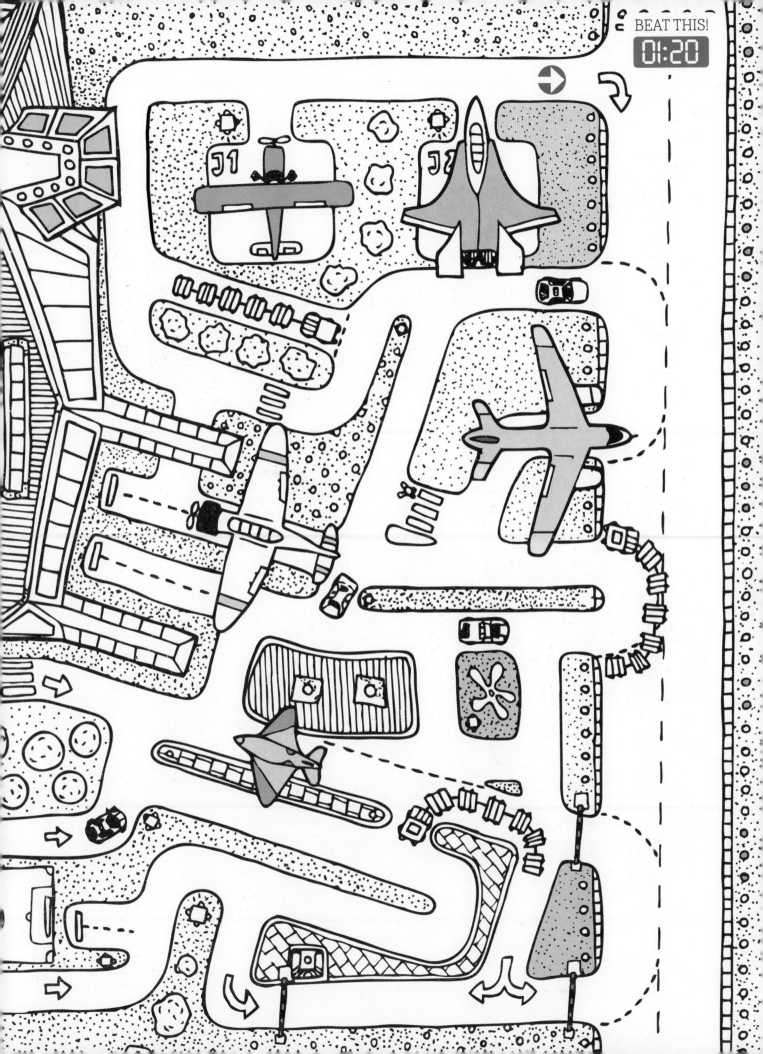

BEAT THIS!
01:20

Don't get in a muddle or lost in the middle!

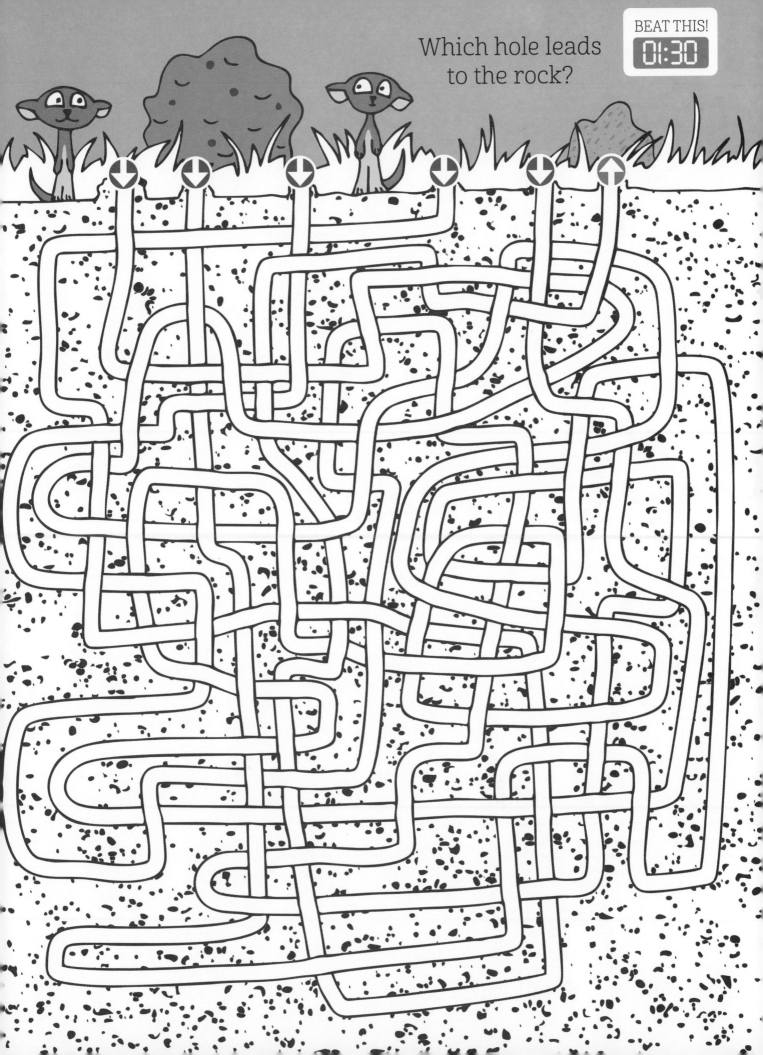

Which hole leads to the rock?

BEAT THIS!
01:30

Which hose is connected
to the faucet?

BEAT THIS!
01:35

?

Get the hamster out the other end of the tubes!

BEAT THIS!

01:55

Find your way through the maze in record time!

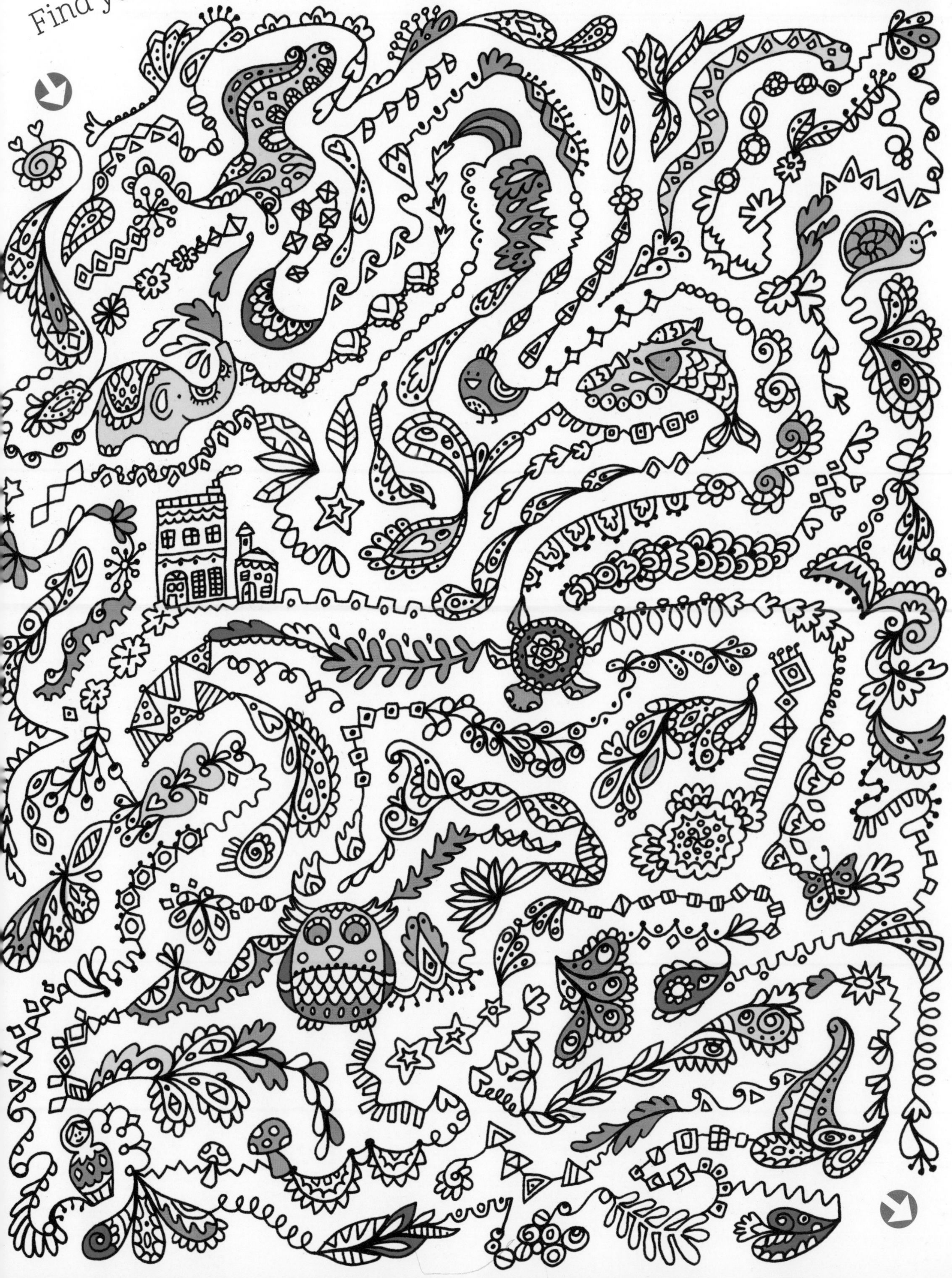

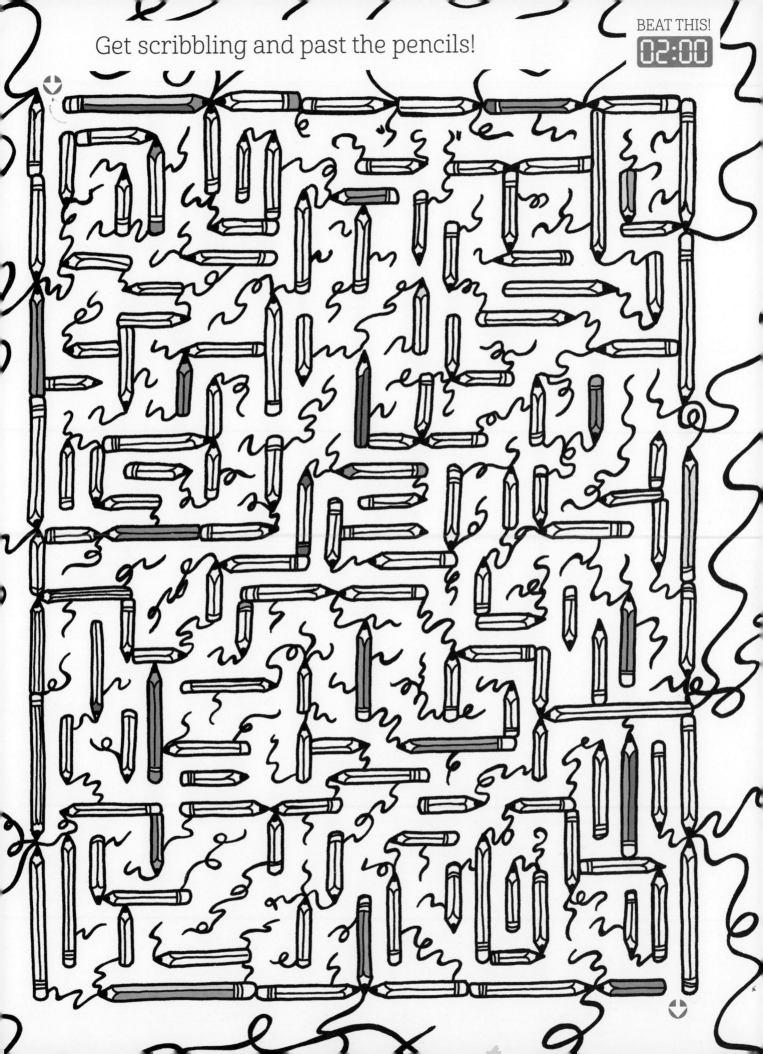

Are you going to be the first in the sea? Let's see!

BEAT THIS!
02:00

Only one route will get you through! But which one?

Don't stop to eat the sweets. Beat the clock!

BEAT THIS!
02:10

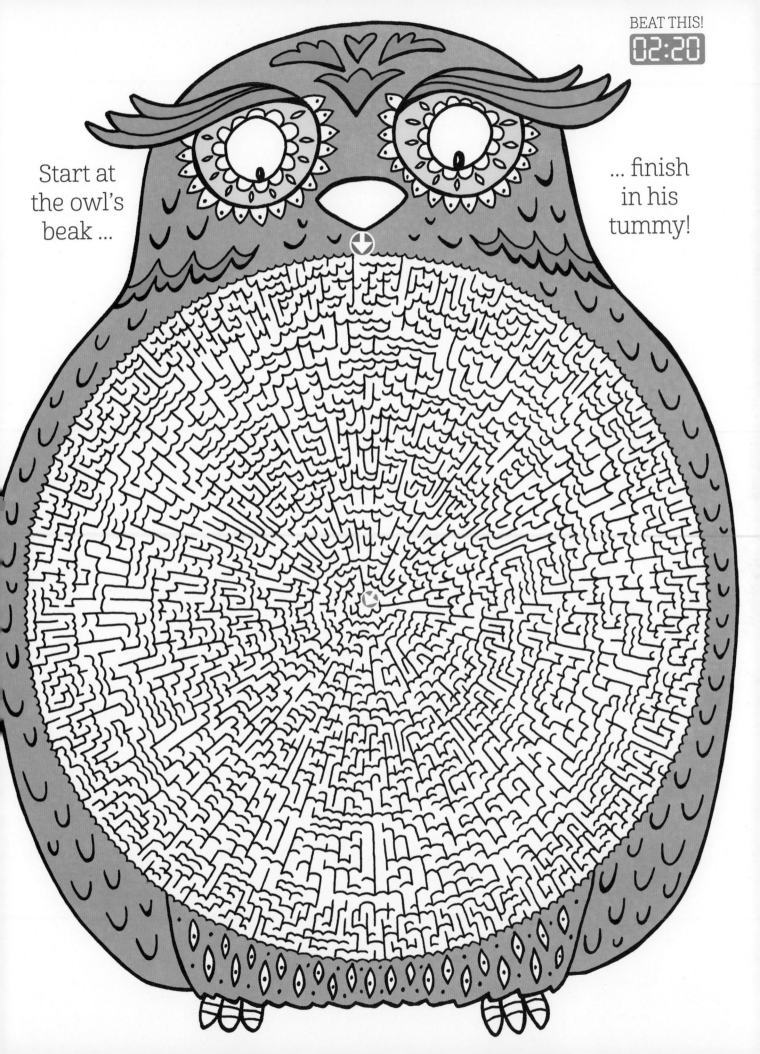

Start at the owl's beak ...

... finish in his tummy!

Loop the loop with the orange plane!

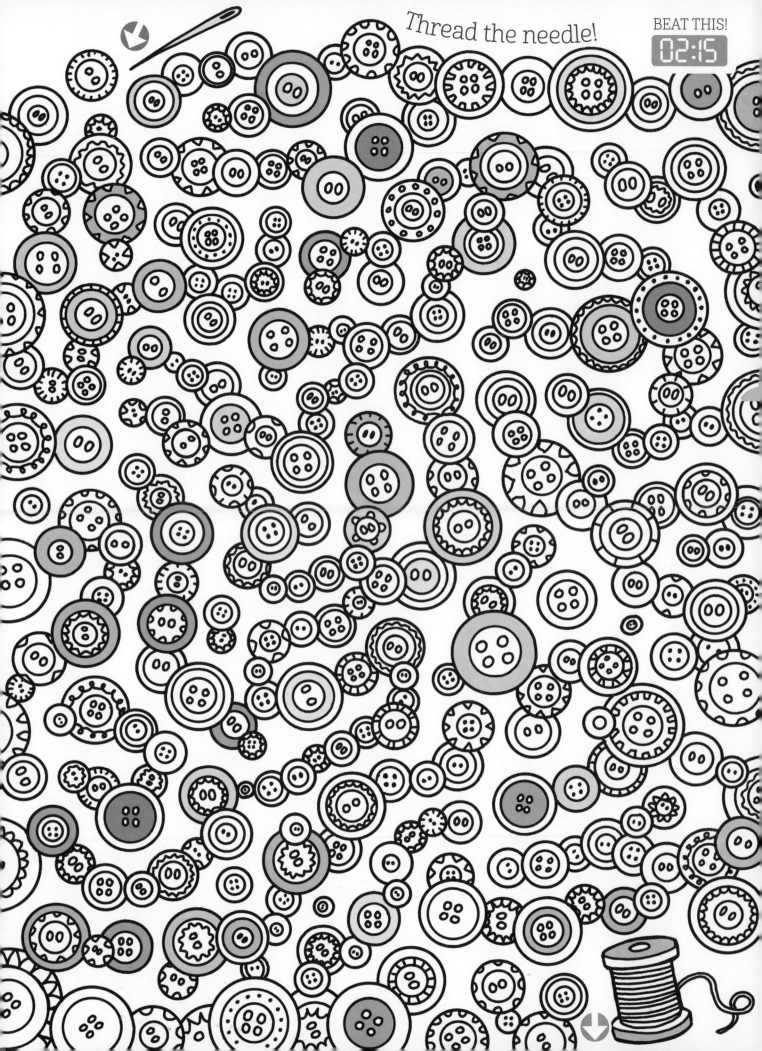

Thread the needle!

BEAT THIS!
02:15

BEAT THIS!
02:15

Munch your way through the apple!

Get in the flow! Which  way does the water go?

Get the crab to the sea!

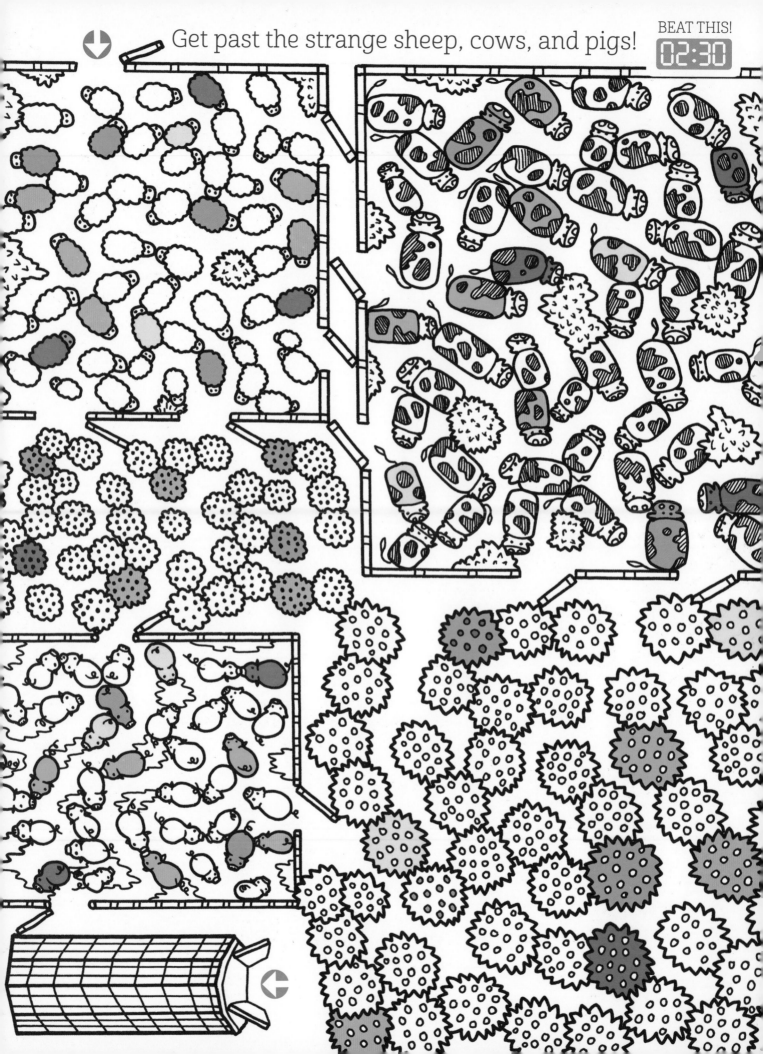

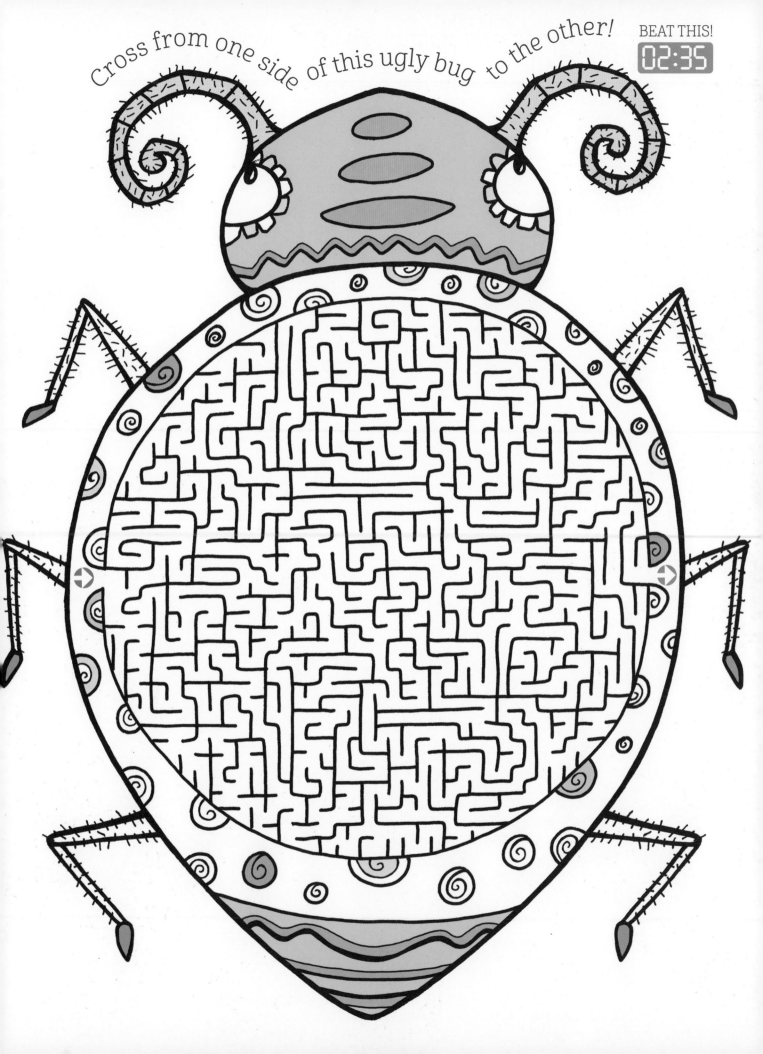

Which way out?

How do you get from the front door to the chimney?

BEAT THIS!
02:45

Choose which route to get to the apple on top of the cake.

BEAT THIS!
02:45

Bee quick! Get to the hive as quickly as you can!

BEAT THIS!
02:50

Which way in?

BEAT THIS!
03:00

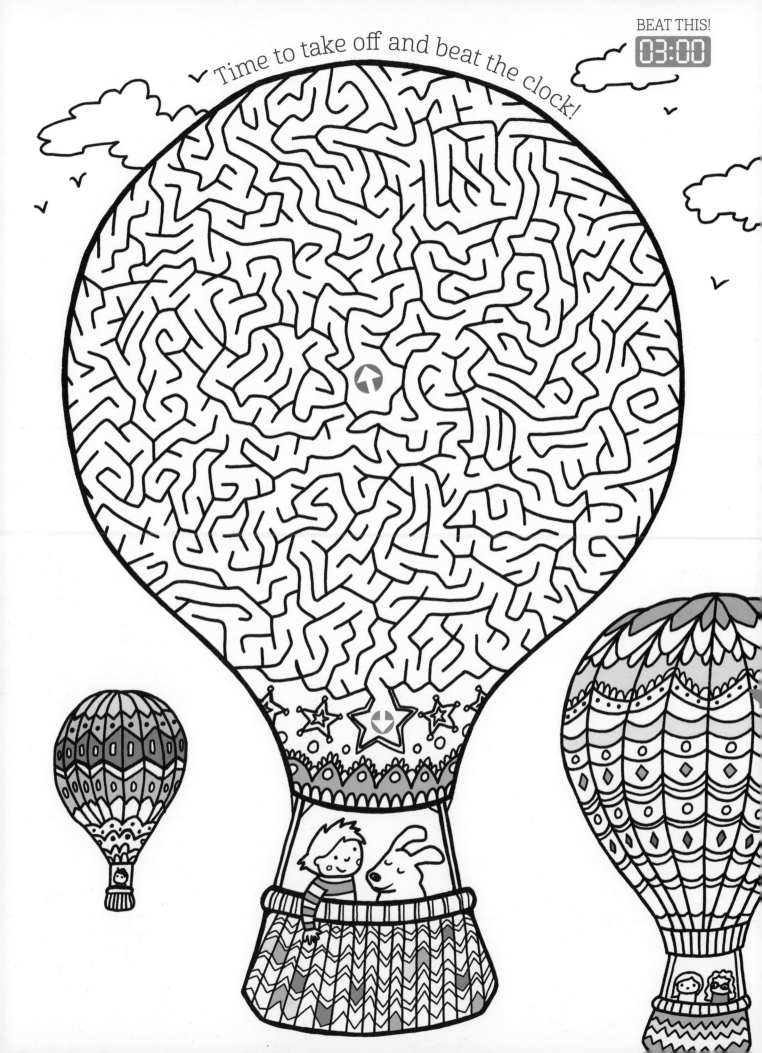

Time to take off and beat the clock!

This building is impossible!
Find your way to one of the doors on this page.

Found the right door? Only one of the doors on this
page will lead you out of the maze!

BEAT THIS!
03:00

The captain of the ship has to get to the engine room. But which is the right way to go?

BEAT THIS!
03:00

It's tricky! Which way? Can you decide?

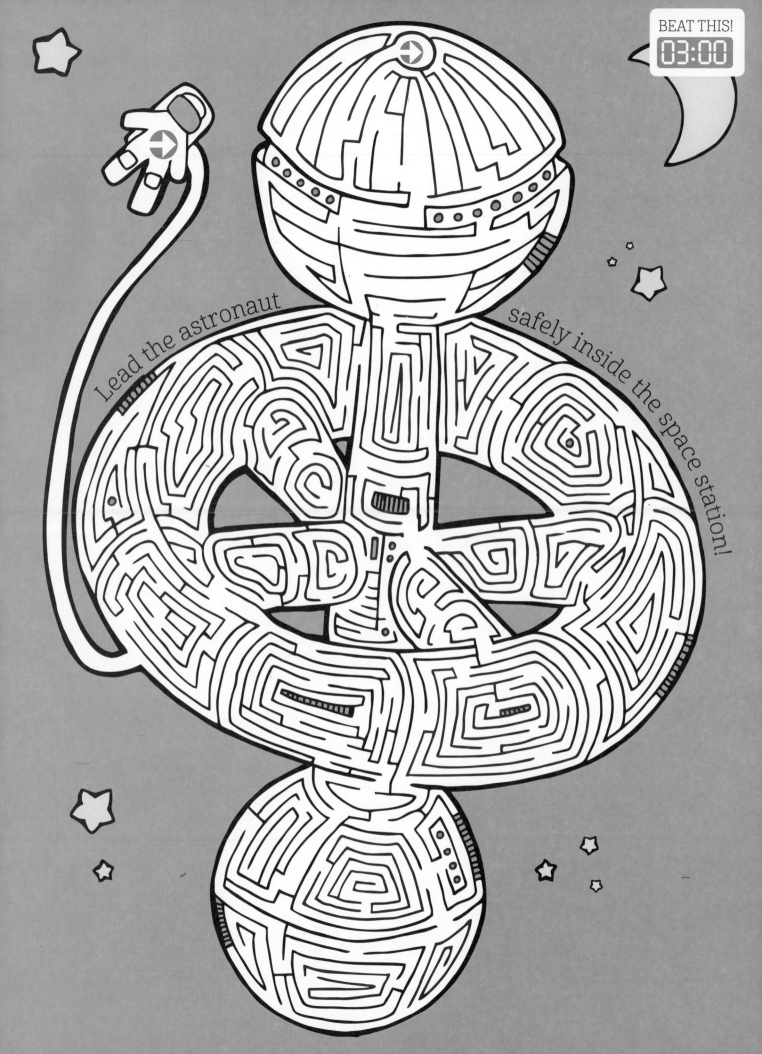

This will really boggle your eyes! Get to the middle!

Find your way out of the splashes to the top of the fountain!

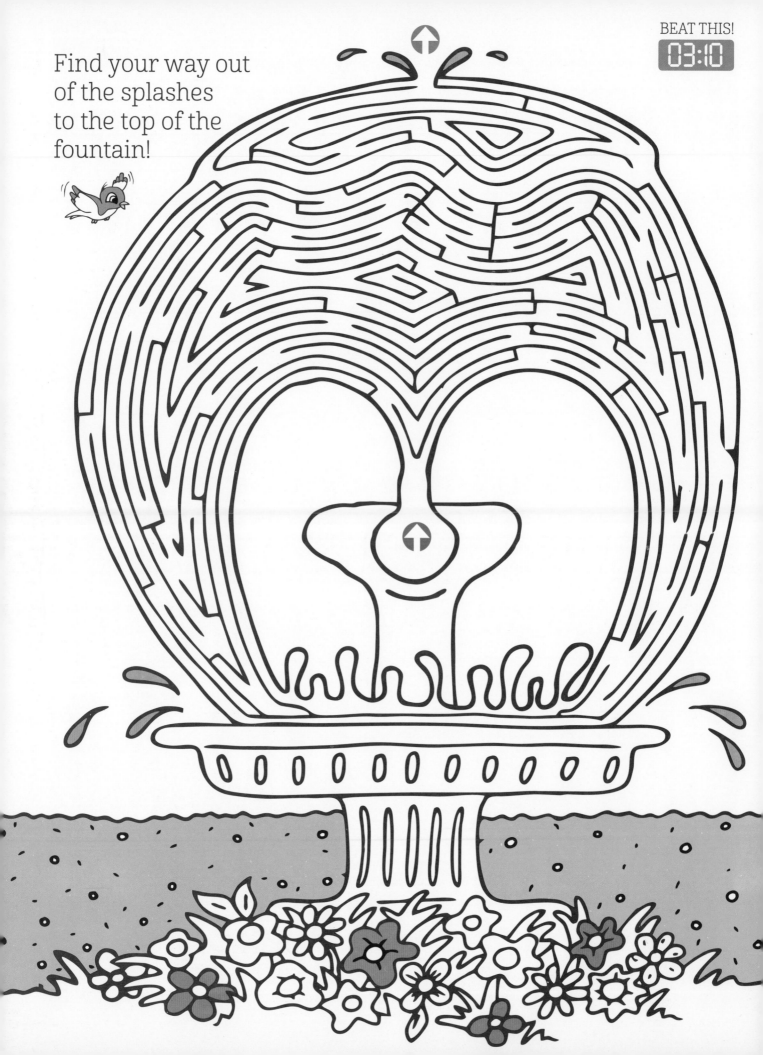

Can you find your way out of the pattern on the turtle's back and beat the clock?

Tip: go through a door to get past the tower!

You're inside a computer! Follow the silver circuits.

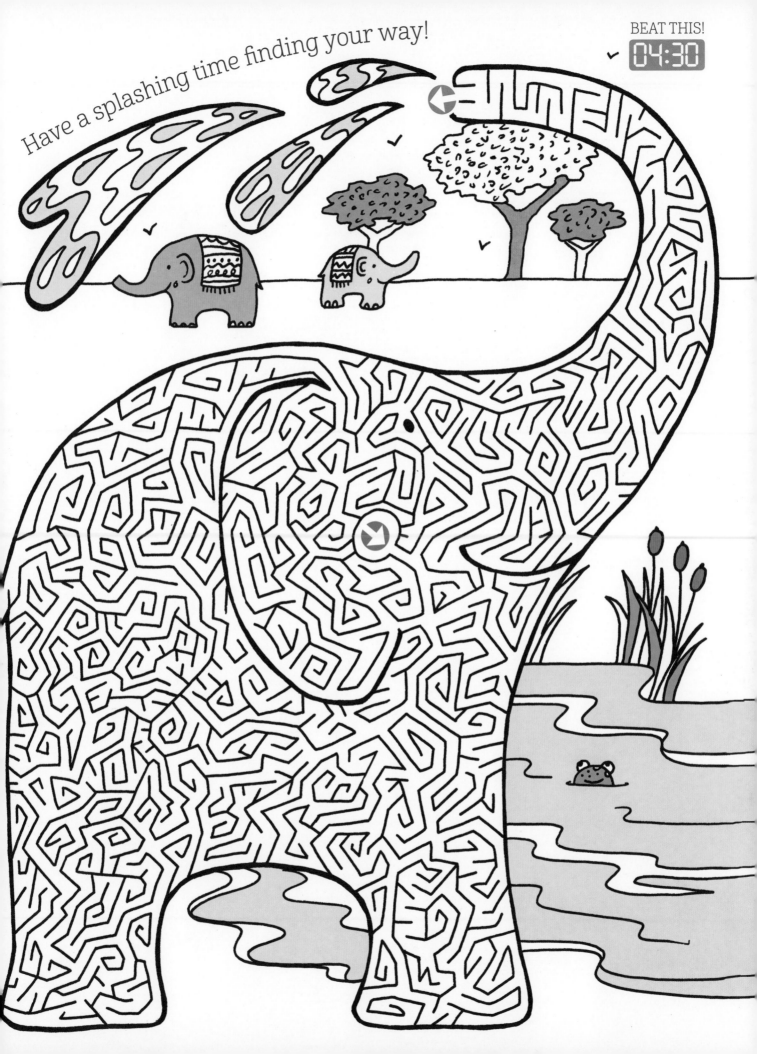

Find a way through my circuits!

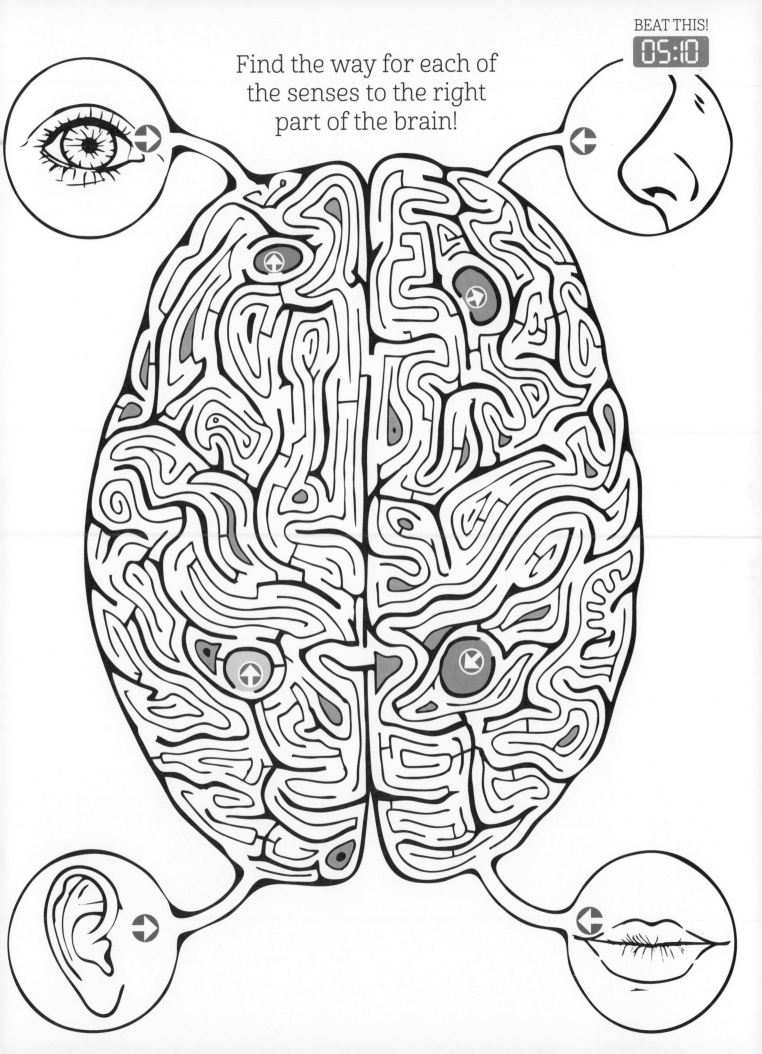

Find the way for each of
the senses to the right
part of the brain!

BEAT THIS!
05:10

Help the bees
find the pretty
flowers!

06:00

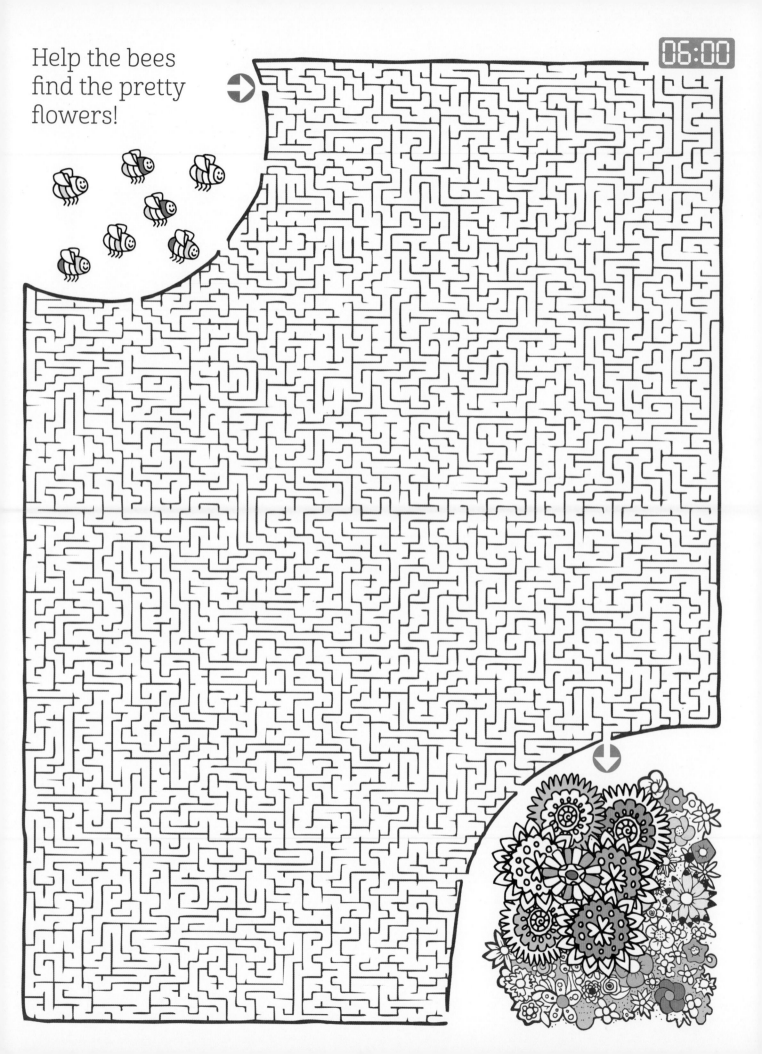

Start on this page.

Find the way that links to a letter on the right-hand page and gets you to the end!

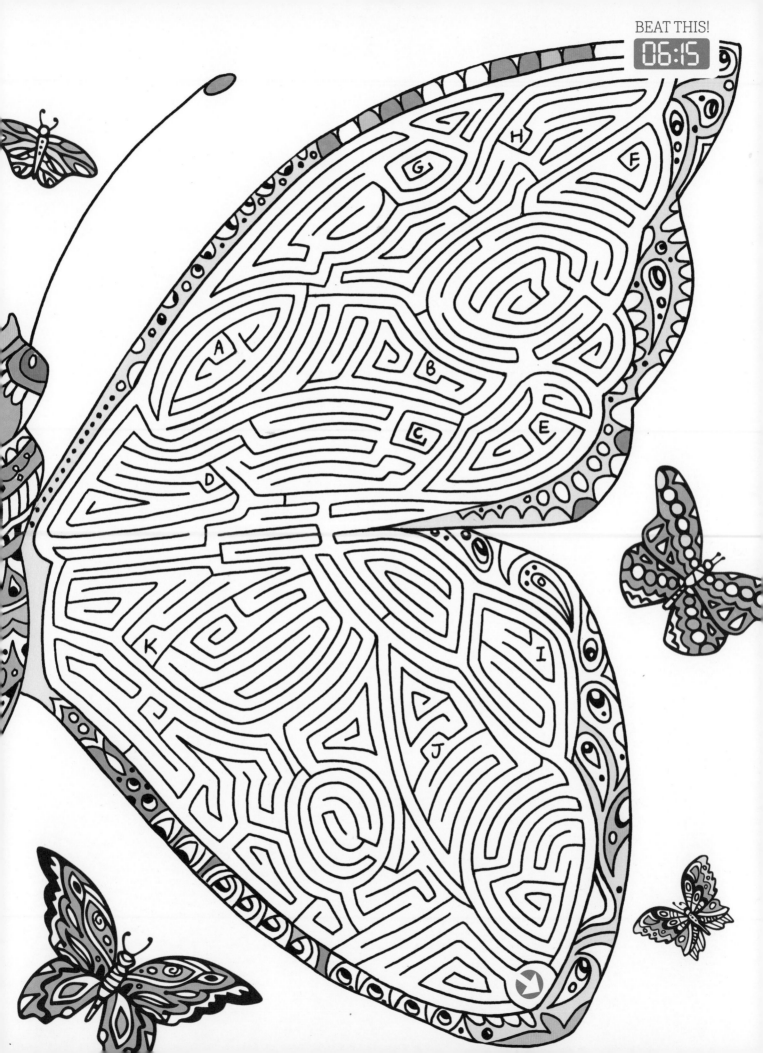

Get the diver to the boat by matching the number on this page to the number on the opposite page.

This one is tricky!

Get on board!

Get the beetles to the flower!

BEAT THIS!
14:15

Here are four mini mazes to finish!
Can you do all four in under two minutes?

Solutions

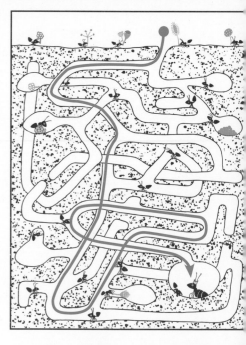
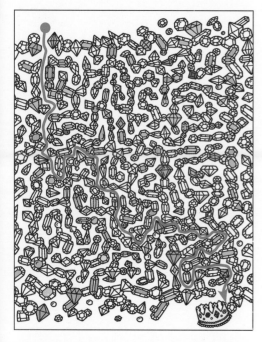
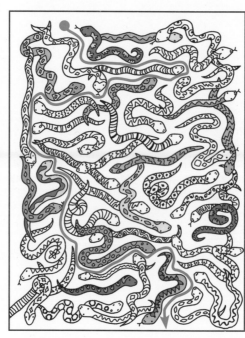

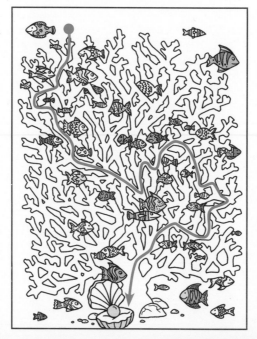

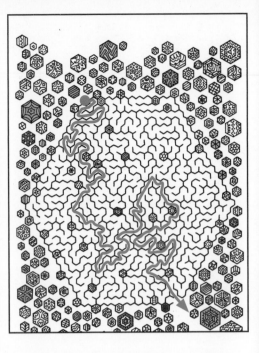
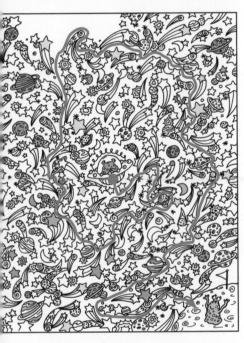

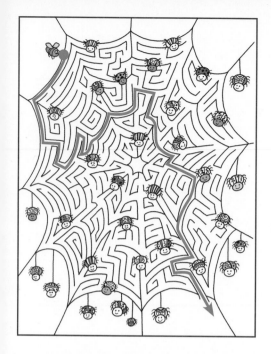
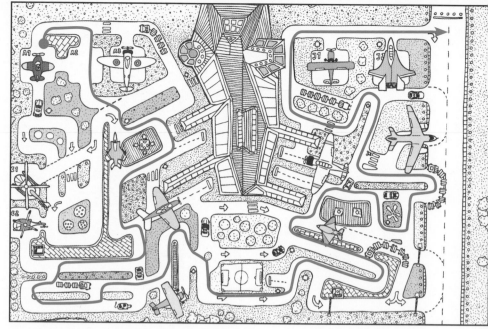
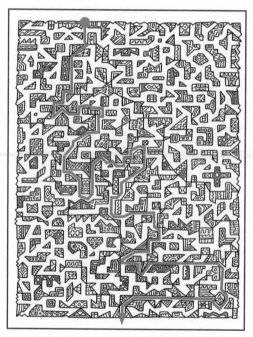
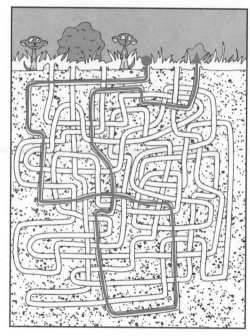

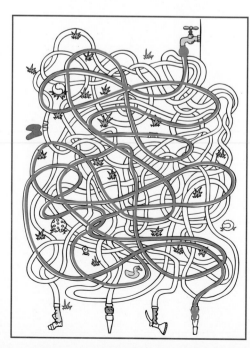
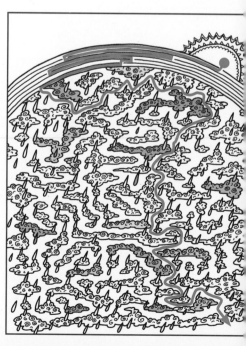

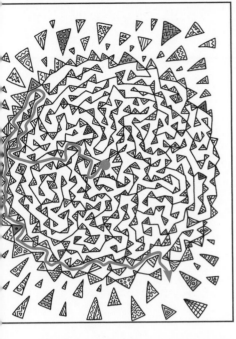

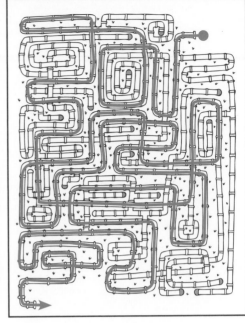

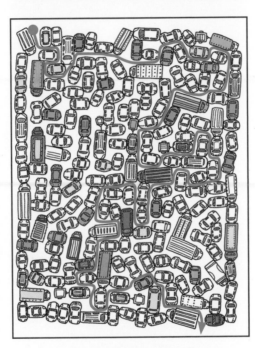
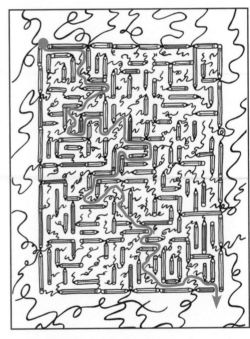

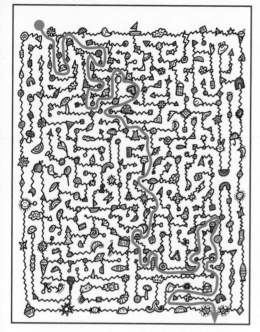

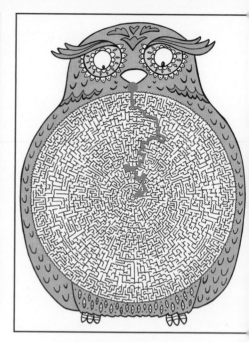

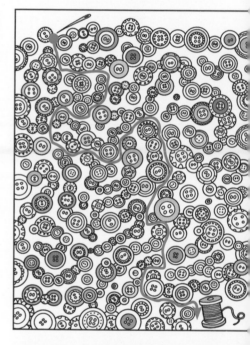

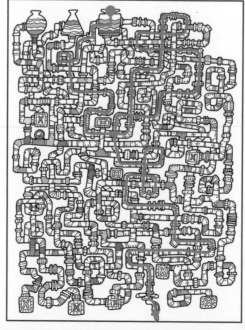
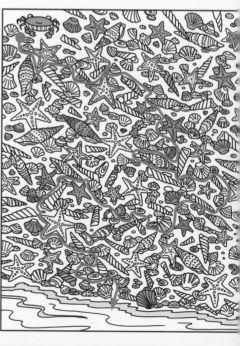

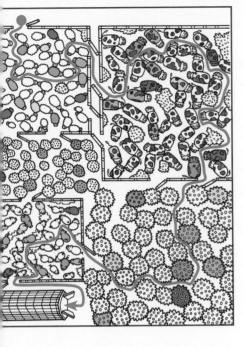
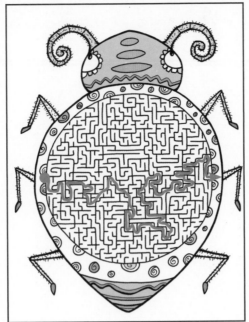

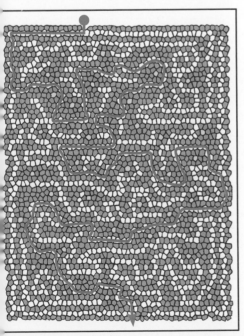

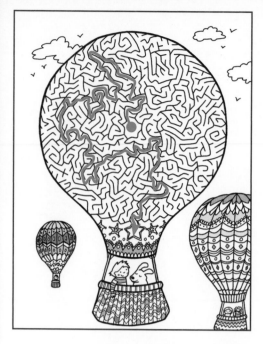

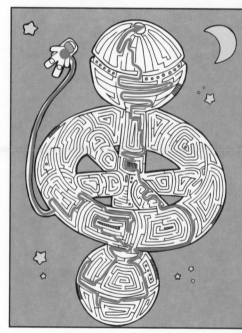

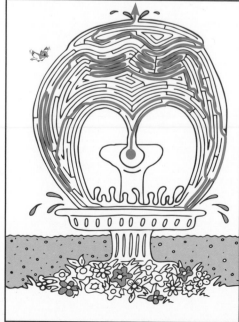

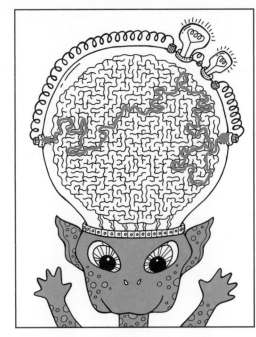
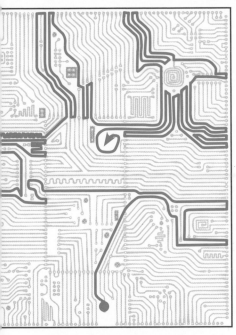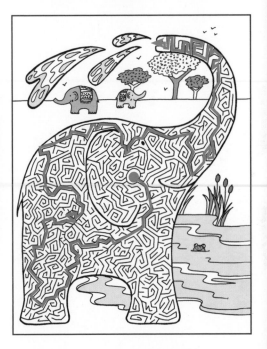
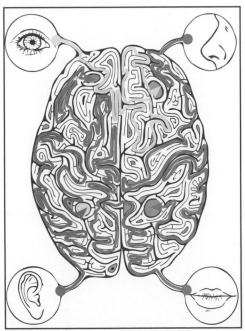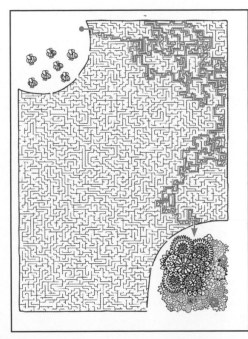

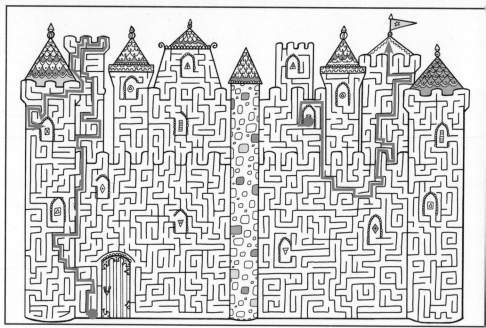